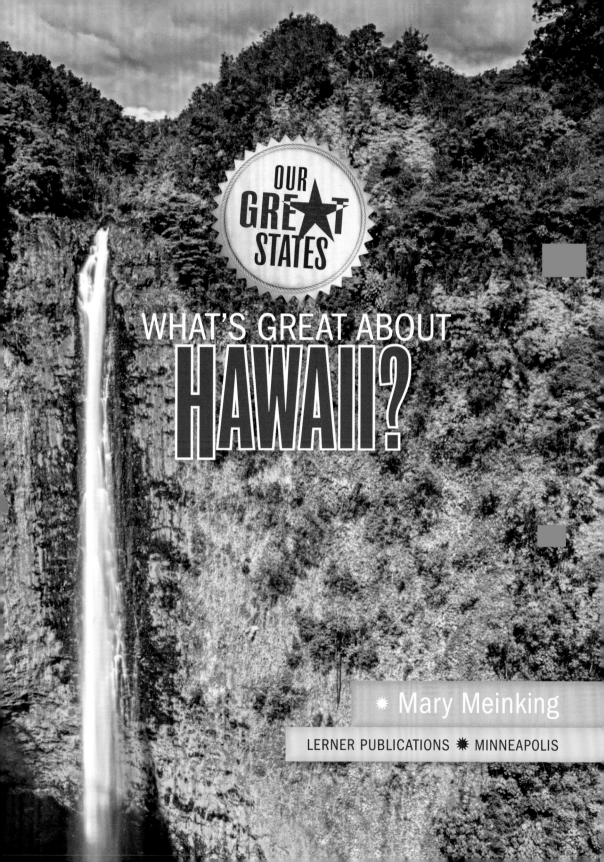

OUR
GRE★T
STATES

WHAT'S GREAT ABOUT

# HAWAII?

✳ Mary Meinking

LERNER PUBLICATIONS ✳ MINNEAPOLIS

# CONTENTS

## HAWAII
# WELCOMES YOU! ✳ 4

Copyright © 2016
by Lerner Publishing Group, Inc.

Content Consultant: John P. Rosa, PhD
Assistant Professor of History
University of Hawai'i at Mānoa

Lerner Publications Company
A division of Lerner Publishing Group, Inc.
241 First Avenue North
Minneapolis, MN 55401 USA

For reading levels and more information, look
up this title at www.lernerbooks.com.

Main body text set in ITC Franklin Gothic Std
Book Condensed 12/15.
Typeface provided by Adobe Systems.

Library of Congress Cataloging-in-Publication
Data

Meinking, Mary.
       What's great about Hawaii? / by Mary
Meinking.
          pages   cm. — (Our great states)
       Includes index.
       Audience: Grades 4-6.
       ISBN 978-1-4677-3887-3 (lb : alk. paper)
       ISBN 978-1-4677-8495-5 (pb : alk. paper)
       ISBN 978-1-4677-8496-2 (EB pdf)
       1. Hawaii—Juvenile literature.  I. Title.
DU623.25.M45 2016
919.6904'42—dc23                2015000975

Manufactured in the United States of America
1 - PC - 7/15/15

# HAWAII Welcomes You!

Hawaii is more than a tropical paradise in the Pacific Ocean. The islands have everything from volcanoes and desert-like craters to rainforests and thundering waterfalls. Bamboo forests and sandy beaches cover other parts of the islands. Hawaii is warm all year. Tourists and locals surf, swim, fish, kayak, tube, and snorkel in the warm water. And there's plenty to do on land. Hawaii is the perfect place to hike, bike, or ride a zip line. And don't forget about all of Hawaii's historic sites. Hawaiian cultural events are great ways to pass the time. Keep reading to learn about the top ten things that make Hawaii great!

PACIFIC OCEAN

KAUAI

NIIHAU

*Anahulu River*

Wahiawa

OAHU

Mililani

Kaneohe

Kailua

Waipahu

Pearl City

Honolulu

N

MOLOKAI

Kahului

MAUI

LANAI

Kihei

MOLOKINI

Haleakala National Park

KAHOOLAWE

Miles

0    20    40    60

0   20   40   60   80

Kilometers

Mauna Kea
(13,796 feet/4,205 m)

*Wailuku River*

Hilo

KAU DESERT

ISLAND OF HAWAII

Hawaii Volcanoes National Park

PACIFIC OCEAN

Explore Hawaii's beaches and all the places in between! Just turn the page to find out all about THE ALOHA STATE. >

# MAUI SURFER GIRLS

> Nothing says "Hawaii" like surfing. The ancient sport of kings and queens began in Hawaii. Try it on any island! Visit Maui Surfer Girls in Lahaina. They can teach you if you've never surfed before. Lessons last for two hours. Your small class will learn the basics on dry land. Then it's time to hit the waves. The waters near the west side of Maui have some of the best waves in Hawaii for beginners.

Out on the water, watch for the perfect wave. Teachers give you a gentle push toward shore. Then it's your turn to paddle. Stand up on the board and ride the wave! Soon you'll be surfing Hawaii's giant 20-foot (6-meter) swells.

You can do more than surf at the beach. Try stand-up paddleboarding, boogie boarding, body surfing, swimming, or building a sandcastle. Or just put on your sunscreen and catch some rays!

## HAWAIIAN ISLANDS

Hawaii is a group of islands in the Pacific Ocean. The islands are made up of volcanic rock. There are more than one hundred islands that spread across 1,500 miles (2,415 kilometers), but only eight are considered main islands. These include Niihau, Kauai, Oahu, Molokai, Lanai, Kahoolawe, Maui, and the Big Island. The Big Island is the largest, but Oahu is the most populated. The state's capital, Honolulu, is on Oahu.

See how many waves you can catch on your boogie board!

# HALEAKALA NATIONAL PARK

> Visit the massive Haleakala National Park on Maui. Rising high above you is the rocky summit of a dormant volcano. Haleakala towers 10,023 feet (3,055 m) above sea level. Dress warmly when you visit Haleakala's summit. The mountain reaches the clouds where the air is cold! The chilly peak is most colorful at sunrise or sunset. You can see five other Hawaiian islands from the summit on a clear day.

Join a ranger-led hike. You'll go in and around the volcano. The park has 37 miles (60 km) of hiking trails. Join the Citizen Scientist Project or the Junior Ranger Program. You'll learn about nature and earn badges.

Take a trip to the Kipahulu District. This is Haleakala's tropical side. The area is also known as Oheʻo Gulch or the Seven Sacred Pools. There are more than seven pools, though. Hike the 4-mile (6 km) Pipiwai Trail. It passes over streams and through a bamboo forest. The streams flow over two waterfalls.

Watch out for sharp rocks while swimming in the Seven Sacred Pools.

Be on the lookout for the state bird, the nene, at Haleakala National Park.

# MOLOKINI SNORKEL & WHALE WATCH

> Many beaches around the Hawaiian Islands are great for snorkeling. Snorkel in the sunken volcanic crater Molokini, near Maui. You can only get to Molokini by boat. Maui Snorkel Charters takes visitors there.

The four-hour trip begins early in the morning. The waters are calmer then and you can see more fish. Enjoy breakfast on the short boat ride. Then get into your gear. You'll wear a wet suit, a snorkel, flippers, and a floatation device. Take a snorkel lesson before you jump in. Once you're in the water, look for more than 250 species of fish that surround you.

Snorkel again on the other side of the island. See a shipwreck and Turtle Town. Turtle Town is a protected area where many green sea turtles live. Try to visit between January and April. That's when you can see whales and dolphins in the area. Stop snorkeling and watch humpback whales in the wild.

Sometimes turtles swim right up to snorkelers in Turtle Town.

## WHALING

In the early 1800s, people hunted whales for their blubber, or fat. Whale blubber was boiled down to make oil. The oil burned in lamps and greased machinery. The best hunting grounds for whales were around Japan. Whaling ships began stopping in Hawaii in 1819 to restock their ships for the long trip to Japan. Eventually, hunters caught too many whales. There were not many left in the ocean. Today whales are protected from most hunting.

# HAWAII VOLCANOES NATIONAL PARK

Take a stroll through the underground Nahuku-Thurston Lava Tube. This tunnel was formed by flowing hot lava!

> There are five volcanoes on Hawaii's Big Island. You can see Kilauea and Mauna Loa in action at Hawaii Volcanoes National Park. Stop at the Kilauea Visitor Center to find out if and where the lava is flowing that day. Then walk next door to the Sulphur Banks. Steam escapes between crystal-covered rocks. The sulfur smells like rotten eggs.

Visit the Jaggar Museum. Peek through the telescopes on the observation deck. You'll see the Kilauea caldera up close. Inside the museum is a seismograph. It monitors the volcanoes to predict when they'll erupt.

There are more than 150 miles (240 km) of hiking trails in the park. The air is hot and dry in some places. In others it is wet like a rain forest. You might see lava pouring into the ocean. Walk through the Nahuku-Thurston Lava Tube. The tube is made of hardened lava and used to carry a river of hot red lava through it.

## PELE, VOLCANO GODDESS

Ancient Hawaiians believed the goddess Pele lived in Kilauea Volcano. The legend said she made the volcano erupt when she became angry. Eruptions destroyed roads and villages. Pele was the goddess of fire, the maker of mountains, the melter of rock, and the eater of forests. Many modern Hawaiians still believe in Pele.

# MOKUPAPAPA DISCOVERY CENTER

> You don't have to get wet to explore Hawaii's coral reefs. The Mokupapapa Discovery Center for Hawaii's Remote Coral Reefs is in Hilo. This free aquarium teaches about the 1,200 miles (1,930 km) of fragile coral reefs in the ocean north of the island Kauai. The reefs are part of the Papahanaumokuakea Marine National Monument. Coral reefs are home to more than 7,000 species of animals. Many marine mammals, fish, sea turtles, birds, and invertebrates live in the reefs.

In the giant aquarium you'll see thousands of colorful fish. They swim near a living coral reef. Check out the interactive displays. There are 3-D models of local animals and life-size wildlife statues. Watch a movie about marine life in the theater. You can even operate a submarine's robotic arm.

The Moorish Idol fish is one of the thousands of fish you can see near Hawaii's coral reefs.

# MOUNTAIN TUBING

The tunnels at Kauai Backcountry Adventure were hand dug more than one hundred years ago to carry water for crops.

> If you're looking for adventure, stop at Kauai Backcountry Adventure in Hanamaulu. Here you can tube on a former plantation's river. Grab an inner tube, gloves, and a headlamp and hop in a truck. Your guide will take you deep into the rain forest. Listen to facts and stories about the island and the plantation's history.

When you arrive at the launch site, wade into the river and sit down in your tube. Then let gravity do the rest! You'll float through canals, tunnels, and flumes.

Enjoy the views as you float. Don't forget to turn on your headlamp in the tunnels! Shout as loud as you can and listen to your voice echo off the cave walls! At the end of your ride, enjoy a picnic lunch provided by the tour. You can also swim in a natural swimming hole.

## IRRIGATION

Early Hawaiians knew how to move water from streams to their fields. Plants such as sugar cane and taro need lots of water. In 1856, settlers constructed the Rice Ditch on Kauai to transport water. Other systems followed. These systems helped the sugar industry boom in Hawaii for more than 150 years. Sugar helped the state's economy grow.

# PRINCEVILLE RANCH

**Soar through the treetops at Princeville Ranch.**

> Try many activities during your visit to the island of Kauai. The Jungle Valley Adventure at Princeville Ranch has it all. Wear a swimsuit under comfy clothes, along with sturdy shoes that can get muddy and wet. You'll be hiking through rain forests and kayaking in rivers.

Start with a beginner kayak trip on the Kalihiwai Stream. Paddle the gentle waters as you take in the sights and sounds of the rain forest around you. Tie up your kayak and follow your guide on a hike deeper into the rain forest. You'll cross streams, mountain valleys, and a ridge covered in ferns. Your guide will point out plants and animals along the way. Learn about Hawaiian history and legends with every step.

Next, head over to the zip lines. Strap into a harness and choose between the two 400-foot (122 m) runs. When you've reached the other side, cross a bridge to find twin waterfalls and a swimming hole. Jump in or float on an inner tube before enjoying a picnic lunch!

Cool off in the refreshing swimming hole near Kalihiwai Stream.

# HONOLULU ZOO

> Get close to more than nine hundred animals at the Honolulu Zoo. You'll see Komodo dragons, orangutans, lemurs, and more. Make your way to the African Savanna exhibit. Listen for elephants trumpeting or lions roaring. Then watch baboons and chimpanzees swing from the trees. Head to the Keiki Zoo exhibit. Here you can crawl through tunnels and play with water wheels. You can also pet turtles, pigs, goats, and a llama!

You may want to sign up for a Dinner Safari. You'll get to tour the zoo after it closes. What do the animals do at night? You'll find out! Enjoy a delicious dinner before visiting some of the nocturnal animals. Then roast a marshmallow over a campfire. Listen for all of the animal sounds. The zoo never sleeps!

Be sure to find the llama
in the Keiki Zoo exhibit.

Watch the lemurs cuddle
at the Honolulu Zoo.

# POLYNESIAN CULTURAL CENTER

> Visit seven Pacific islands without leaving the Polynesian Cultural Center in Laie on the island of Oahu. Many Hawaii residents are descended from Polynesians. Polynesians come from many islands in the east-central Pacific Ocean. You'll learn all about Tonga, Tahiti, Samoa, and other Polynesian islands. See how Polynesians dress, what they eat, and hear the music they listen to. Learn to make a fire, throw a spear, race boats, fish, or drum. You can fill out a Passport to Polynesia activity booklet. Turn in the completed book for a special prize.

After a busy day, enjoy a luau of Polynesian food. There are three yummy menus to choose from. You'll feel like royalty in your flower lei as you watch the evening show. It includes live music and hula dances that tell stories.

## THE HULA

Early Hawaiians did not have a written language. Instead, they remembered their people's past through the hula dance. It was important not to change the steps or chants. In ancient times, men performed the hula during religious ceremonies. Women took over dancing when men went to war. Modern Hawaiians still dance the hula at luaus across the Hawaiian Islands.

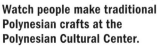

**Watch people make traditional Polynesian crafts at the Polynesian Cultural Center.**

# DOLE PINEAPPLE PLANTATION

> Visit the Dole Pineapple Plantation in Wahiawa on Oahu for a sweet treat. You can sample the golden fruit. James Drummond Dole opened the plantation in 1900. He was not the first to grow pineapples in Hawaii, but he eventually became known as the Pineapple King. These days, visitors can explore the whole plantation.

Hop aboard the Pineapple Express train. This twenty-minute guided tour will take you on a 2-mile (3.2 km) journey of the plantation. After your ride, put on your running shoes. The plantation has the world's largest maze. Make your way through the 3.1 miles (5 km) of paths. If you find the eight secret stations and finish first in your group, you win a prize. Be sure to also join a Plantation Garden Tour. You'll see tropical crops including coffee.

## YOUR TOP TEN

You've just read about ten awesome things to see and do in Hawaii. Now it's your turn! If you visited Hawaii, what would be on your Top Ten list? What places in Hawaii do you really want to visit? Grab a piece of paper and jot down your Hawaii Top Ten list. You could even make it into a book. Use your own drawings or pictures that you find on the Internet.

Learn more about Hawaii's history on the Pineapple Express.

See up close how a pineapple grows in the plantation gardens!

KAUAI

NIIHAU

Kauai Backcountry
Adventures
(Hanamaulu)

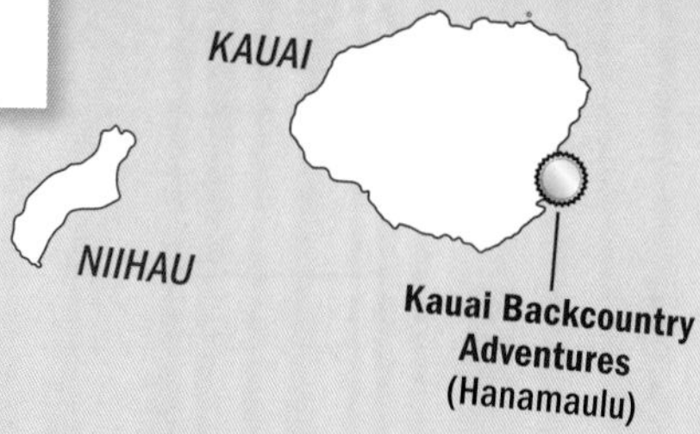

## > MAP KEY

⭐ Capital city

○ City

○ Point of interest

▲ Highest elevation

Visit www.lerneresource.com to learn
more about the state flag of Hawaii.

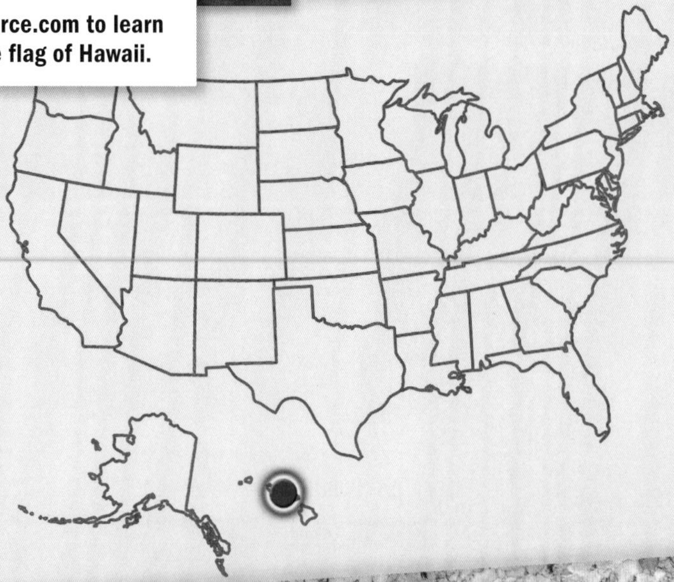

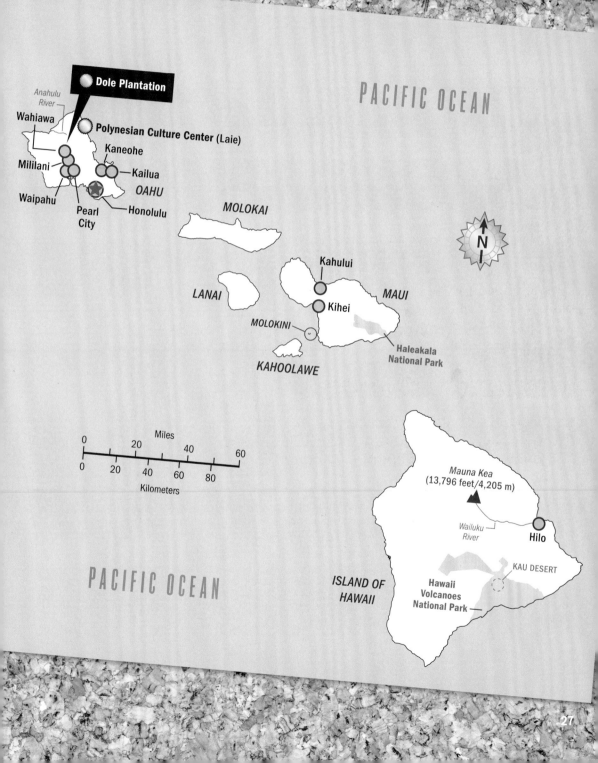

Dole Plantation

*Anahulu River*

Wahiawa

Polynesian Culture Center (Laie)

Mililani

Kaneohe

Kailua

Waipahu

OAHU

Pearl City

Honolulu

PACIFIC OCEAN

N

MOLOKAI

LANAI

Kahului

Kihei

MAUI

MOLOKINI

Haleakala National Park

KAHOOLAWE

Miles

0   20   40   60

0   20   40   60   80

Kilometers

Mauna Kea
(13,796 feet/4,205 m)

*Wailuku River*

Hilo

PACIFIC OCEAN

ISLAND OF HAWAII

KAU DESERT

Hawaii Volcanoes National Park

27

# HAWAII FACTS

**NICKNAME:** The Aloha State

**SONG:** "Hawaii Ponoi" by King Kalakaua

**MOTTO:** *Ua mau ke ea o ka 'aina i ka pono,* or "The life of the land is perpetuated in righteousness"

> **FLOWER:** yellow hibiscus

**TREE:** kukui (candlenut tree)

**BIRD:** nene (Hawaiian goose)

> **ANIMAL:** humpback whale

**DATE AND RANK OF STATEHOOD:** August 21, 1959; the 50th State

> **CAPITAL:** Honolulu

**AREA:** 6,468 square miles (16,752 sq. km)

**AVERAGE JANUARY TEMPERATURE:** 68°F (20°C)

**AVERAGE JULY TEMPERATURE:** 75°F (24°C)

**POPULATION AND RANK:** 1,404,054; 40th (2013)

**MAJOR CITIES AND POPULATIONS:** Honolulu (387,170), Pearl City (47,698), Hilo (43,263), Kailua (38,635), Waipahu (38,216)

**NUMBER OF US CONGRESS MEMBERS:** 2 representatives, 2 senators

**NUMBER OF ELECTORAL VOTES:** 4

**NATURAL RESOURCES:** fish, flowers, coral, pearls, sand, papayas, passion fruit, potatoes, taro

> **AGRICULTURAL PRODUCTS:** coffee, macadamia nuts, pineapples, sugar

**MANUFACTURED GOODS:** concrete products, food products, petroleum products, printed materials

**STATE HOLIDAYS AND CELEBRATIONS:** King Kamehameha I Day

# GLOSSARY

**caldera:** a large crater formed by an explosion

**crater:** the area on top of a volcano that is bowl-shaped

**dormant:** not active

**flume:** a deep channel of water

**hula:** a traditional Hawaiian dance

**invertebrate:** any animal that lacks a backbone

**lei:** a necklace made of flowers

**luau:** a traditional meal and celebration in Hawaii

**nocturnal:** active mainly during the night

**seismograph:** a machine that measures the motion of the ground and predicts earthquakes and eruptions

**swell:** an upward and downward movement of ocean water

**taro:** a tropical plant with a thick root that can be boiled and eaten

LERNER

SOURCE™

Expand learning beyond the printed book. Download free, complementary educational resources for this book from our website, www.lerneresource.com.

# FURTHER INFORMATION

Drury-Wagner, Kathryn. *Hawaii's Strangest, Ickiest, Wildest Book Ever!* Honolulu, HI: Mutual Pub., 2013. Learn weird and gross facts about the 50th state's animals, nature, and history.

**Haleakala National Park For Kids**
http://home.nps.gov/hale/forkids/index.htm
Learn about the Hawaiian alphabet, Hawaiian myths, plants, animals, and geology, and even fill in coloring sheets of local wildlife.

**Hawaii Volcanoes National Park For Kids**
http://www.nps.gov/havo/forkids/index.htm
Learn about all the fun things for kids to do in this national park and become a WebRanger.

Lüsted, Marcia Amidon. *Hawaii: The Aloha State*. New York: PowerKids Press, 2011. Explore Hawaii's landmarks, natural wonders, and historical sites.

**Papahānaumokuākea Marine National Monument**
http://www.papahanaumokuakea.gov/education/for_kids.html
Learn about this unique national monument through games, puzzles, coloring pages, and videos.

Walker, Sally M. *Volcanoes*. Minneapolis: Lerner Publications, 2008. Learn how volcanoes form, where they're found, and what happens when they erupt.

# INDEX

## PHOTO ACKNOWLEDGMENTS

The images in this book are used with the permission of: © Roger Nichol/Shutterstock Images, p. 1; NASA, pp. 2–3; © Laura Westlund/Independent Picture Service, pp. 5 (top), 26; © Lorcel/Shutterstock Images, p. 5 (bottom); © Deborah Kolb/Shutterstock Images, p. 4; © Bill Brooks/Alamy, pp. 6–7; © Philip Dyer/iStockphoto, p. 7 (bottom); Jacques Descloitres/NASA Goddard Space Flight Center, p. 7 (top); © Eric Titcombe CC 2.0, pp. 8–9; © Charles Starrett CC 2.0, p. 9 (top); © Michael J. Thompson/Shutterstock Images, p. 9 (bottom); © Forest and Kim Starr CC 2.0, pp. 10–11; © David Fleetham/Alamy, p. 11 (top); Underwood & Underwood/Library of Congress, p. 11 (bottom) (LC-USZ62-40142); © Colleen McNeil CC 2.0, pp. 12–13; © Stephan Hoerold/iStockphoto, p. 12; © Pavel Tvrdy/Shutterstock Images, p. 13; © Lindsey Kramer/US Fish and Wildlife Service, pp. 14–15; © Steven Bates/iStockphoto, p. 15; © Steve Bly/Alamy, pp. 16–17, 16; Library of Congress, p. 17 (LC-USZ62-108293); © Douglas Peebles/Danita Delimont Photography/Newscom, pp. 18–19, 19; © Kristin Jackson/MCT/Newscom, p. 18; © Daniel Ramirez CC 2.0, pp. 20–21, 21 (right), 22–23; © Cliff CC 2.0, p. 21 (left); © RosalreneBetancourt 3/Alamy, p. 23 (bottom); © Boykov/Shutterstock Images, p. 23 (top); © slobo/iStockphoto, pp. 24–25; © randychiu CC 2.0, p. 25 (top); © Jennifer Boyer CC 2.0, p. 25 (bottom); © nicoolay/iStockphoto, p. 26; © nuwatphoto/iStockphoto, p. 29 (top); © adwalsh/iStockphoto, p. 29 (middle left); © jewhyte/iStockphoto, p. 29 (middle right); © blowbackphoto/iStockphoto, p. 29 (bottom).

Front cover: © David Olsen/Getty Images (hula); © iStockphoto.com/jcarillet (hikers); © Kristin Scholtz/ASP/Getty Images (surfer); © Laura Westlund/Independent Picture Service (map); © iStockphoto.com/fpm (seal); © iStockphoto.com/vicm (pushpins); © iStockphoto.com/benz190 (cork board).